THE EMPATHIC INFJ

Awareness and Understanding for the Intuitive Clairsentient

JENNIFER SOLDNER

The Empathic INFJ:

Awareness and Understanding for the

Intuitive Clairsentient

First Edition

© 2015 Jennifer Soldner

All rights reserved.

ISBN 978-1-514-76538-8

Dedicated to my husband,
whose loving support and lending ear
helped me discover who I am
and gave me the courage to write about it.

Other books by
JENNIFER SOLDNER

A Look Inside a Rare Mind:
An INFJ's Journal through Personal Discovery

The Empathic INFJ Workbook:
Tools and Strategies for the Intuitive Clairsentient

AUTHOR'S NOTE

Years ago, when I first discovered that I was an INFJ personality type, I embarked on a journey of self-discovery, finally finding the reason why I struggled so much throughout my life. I documented much of my journey in my partial memoirs, *A Look Inside a Rare Mind*.

While a great deal of my research on my newly discovered type helped me understand myself, I still felt as though something was missing. There was an aspect of my existence that none of the Myers-Briggs descriptions seemed to fit. That is when my research led me to the term *empath*, or clairsentient, where my eyes were opened even further and a new journey of self-discovery began.

After learning about these identifying terms as well as understanding and accepting the unique traits of being an empathic INFJ, my life changed dramatically. I was able to embrace my differences, accept my struggles and flourish in my abilities to cope with areas that previously left me drowning.

Much of my writing is geared toward living as an empathic INFJ and, after being contacted by many others just like me asking for help in all the areas in which I recall struggling, I decided it was time to take the information I learned through my years of research and discovery and compose a simple book with the tools and resources to not only understand what it means to be an empathic INFJ, but also to offer practical solutions to handling everyday living.

My hope is that, when paired with *The Empathic INFJ Workbook: Tools and Strategies for the Intuitive Clairsentient*, you will be able to find awareness and understanding of why you perceive the world so much differently than those around you and how you can harness your abilities and begin truly living out your calling.

Thank you for allowing me to be a part of your journey through self-discovery!

— CONTENTS —

INTRODUCTION

Blake[1] awoke one Tuesday morning, eager to begin his work day, just as he does five times a week. He enjoys a quiet morning, sipping his coffee and readying himself, content with the thoughts casually strolling through his mind. An introvert, Blake feels most comfortable and confident within the walls of his mind, charging his mental batteries to tackle another day. All feels well as he grabs his jacket and briefcase and heads out the door.

---

[1] All names and characters mentioned are fictitious. Any similarity to a real person is merely coincidental.

Once in his car, Blake backs out toward the road, pausing for the line of commuters to give way to a break. Soon he is on the road, amidst a whole flock of people he has never before met, all on their way to beginning their days.

So sure of himself moments before, Blake begins to stagger a little in his thoughts. His emotions start to confusingly shift from peaceful and content to frustrated, then anxious, then angry. He logically cannot understand the source of these new emotions, but allows them to alter his thinking. The work day he was just looking forward to is suddenly riddled with negative emotions, leaving him feeling nothing but dread to arrive at his desk.

The rest of the day, Blake attempts to stay locked away in his cubicle, hoping to tap into his introverted mind and recharge to regain the sense of peace he felt that morning, prior to hitting the road, but to no avail. His emotions leave him feeling drained without even having much human interaction.

The fatigue of handling the negative emotions as well as his self-berating for not being more positive and assured shifts Blake into a pessimistic line of thinking, dragging him down into sadness and loneliness, longing to crawl into his bed and try again tomorrow.

Little does he know, Blake is an empathic INFJ who is unaware of his abilities, leaving him to struggle in a cloud of confusion, frustration and self-loathing day in and day out. This daily cycle goes on, ultimately leaving him depressed and incapable of finding a way out of the downward spiral.

Can you relate to Blake? Do you know what it is like to feel on top of the world, confident and assured only to step outside and feel instantly dragged down, worn out and confused? If so, you too may be an empathic INFJ suffering through the inertia of each day wishing there was a way to find emotional consistency and confidence.

What if I told you that you could gain better control over your emotional state, cleansing yourself of the negativity, freeing your life of constant fatigue and mental confusion and bursting through the fog allowing you to stand firm and confident in the light of a beautiful day?

In this book, I offer descriptions and scientific studies which explain what it means to be an empathic

INFJ, allowing you to learn about what is happening in your body and mind that leaves you feeling so out of control. On top of understanding yourself, this book will give you practical and effective tools and techniques that, with practice and consistency, will lead you toward a life you never knew possible, altering your perception of the yourself and the energetic world around you.

UNDERSTANDING THE EMPATHIC INFJ

WHAT IS AN INFJ?

If you have picked up this book, odds are you are at least mildly aware of what an INFJ is but I wanted to offer a quick overview of the personality type and help you better familiarize yourself with what it means to be an INFJ.

INFJ is an acronym for Introvert, iNtuitive, Feeling and Judicial. It is one of the sixteen personality types defined by Katherine Cook Myers and Isabel Briggs Myers[2] based on their interpretations of Carl

---

[2] The Myers & Briggs Foundation. http://www.myersbriggs.org/ Gainesville, FL. 2015.

Jung's complex data and research. They compiled Jung's four dichotomies – Extrovert and Introvert, Sensing and Intuition, Feeling and Thinking, Judicial and Perceiving – into sixteen easy-to-understand personality types. These personality types give us an understanding of how an individual's brain receives and processes information.

Contrary to the fact that it is referred to as *personality typing*, the Myers-Briggs Type Indicator (MBTI) actually has less to do with one's personality and everything to do with how their brain works from receiving and processing external information to communication preferences.

The INFJ receives information through their primary function, intuitive iNtuition (Ni) and processes it through their secondary function, extroverted Feeling (Fe). They also use introverted Thinking (Ti) as they mentally mature and tend to struggle with their fourth function, extroverted Sensing (Se). Some believe that the fourth function is not necessarily underdeveloped, but rather works efficiently in the subconscious.

Because of this cognitive functional stack, INFJs are often known as being highly sensitive individuals with an amazing level of intuition which they prefer to apply towards the greater good of humanity. Even though their intuition allows them to have a certain level of open-mindedness, the judicial INFJ is very interested in organization, structure and clear paths. They enjoy spending a great deal of time inside of their heads as their introverted nature allows them to energize from within, but their Fe function leaves them yearning to help those around them, pulling them back down to earth and fueling them to be doers as well as dreamers.

As a whole, INFJs thrive on their intuition, using it as the main direction of their thoughts and actions, often times trusting it above all else. Their highly sensitive nature tends to lend itself to the potential to have empathic abilities.

WHAT IS AN EMPATH?

There are a lot of arguments surrounding the term empath and what it actually means. Some take it from a more generic viewpoint and think of an empath as one with a high level of empathy, or the ability to directly relate to how another feels. Others believe that the term empath refers to a much deeper and more unique concept. It has been my experience that most who use the term on a more generic level do so out of lack of knowledge of what it means to truly be an empath.

Numerous studies have been conducted about energy waves and frequencies, heart transmissions, synchronicity and so forth, but we are still left with a general lack of understanding about what empathic abilities truly are. For that reason, there are several opinions on the subject ranging from skeptical to prophetic in nature.

The term empath should not be mistaken with sympathy, which is trying to understand what someone is going through, or even the very similar word empathy, which refers to being *familiar* with what someone else is experiencing. An empath literally feels exactly what someone else feels, even if they have never experienced nor can they relate in any way to what the other person is going through. An empath is not someone who relates to the feelings of another, but rather goes much deeper and actually receives the energy of someone else. Empaths absorb these emotions and energies from those around them, often times unwillingly. These energies then affect the empath as though the situation was actually happening to them. Depending on the closeness of the empath to the other individual depends on the range of which these energies can travel and be received. Usually the energies of someone unfamiliar tend to require the empath to be in close proximity while loved ones may be across the country and still affect the empath.

How these energies are received is still widely debated. One class of people believes that the energies travel in waves, emitted from all objects and people around us. Empaths act as sponges or magnets for these energy waves, absorbing them involuntarily.

Another class feels that this is inaccurate and that empaths do not absorb energy waves but rather reach out and take the energy of another person. Think of an aura extending out, wrapping around another and pulling back whatever energy was in the other's aura. While most do not believe this is a conscious act, this class of people does believe that the empath has more control than just passively absorbing.

The third class believes both of these concepts to be accurate. They think that energies are all around us, clinging to objects and individuals as well as emitting from them. The empath absorbs these energies through waves as well as has the ability, whether voluntarily or involuntarily, to reach out and pull another's energy towards them.

Personally, I belong to the third class. I believe that everything is energy and empaths receive this energy in a myriad of ways, sometimes purposefully and other times without their own control. I also believe empaths are, on the whole, highly sensitive people causing these energies in which we are all submerged to affect their bodies and emotions much more powerfully than the average person. So on top of absorbing higher levels of energies, I believe empaths are also more sensitive to their presence within themselves.

While there are varying degrees of empathic abilities which I will explain further on in this book, there are also different types of empaths. The most commonly known type is the *emotional empath*. This is a person who picks up on the emotional energies of another person, feeling exactly what the other person feels, even if they have never experienced the situation or feeling themselves. A second type is a *physical empath*. Physical empaths absorb energies of physical ailments, diseases or pains. For example, when close to someone with a headache, the physical empath will also feel a headache in the exact same location. There are also those with empathic abilities outside of other human beings. These empaths receive the energies from animals, plants or objects. It is possible to have all of these abilities or only one.

Usually, even if someone has come to understand their empathic self, they can still struggle beyond their awareness of other's emotions and feelings. These are usually empaths that absorb from animals, plants or objects without the awareness that they have this capability.

There are those who hear of empathic abilities and scoff at the idea, stating that it simply is not possible to feel another's emotions. They usually say that the reality is the empath is projecting their perceived emotions onto another during any given situation or that the empath's subconscious is picking up on clues that others tend to miss, allowing them a more complete observation of another's feelings.

While both of these ideas may hold some merit and should not be discounted, they tend to leave the genuine empath, especially those with stronger abilities, feeling as though something is missing in such explanations, knowing full well that there is more to it.

To many empaths, these theories feel more like a dismissal of their gifts or their perceptions of life. Rather than attempting to accept that something is different within the empathic mind, skeptics only dismiss them as observational at best, insane or unstable at worst.

Luckily, to the empath's credit, ample scientific research is beginning to point to theories that may prove their experiences to be accurate. Studying energy waves and their effects on individuals both in the same room as well as across the country is showing that our emotional states emit frequencies on varying levels, sending feelings through the air and affecting other individuals who are open to these frequencies. There was actually a study[3] conducted by Rupert Sheldrake, author of *Dogs That Know When Their Owners Are Coming Home: And Other*

---

[3] Sheldrake, Rupert, and Pamela Smart. "A Dog That Seems to Know When His Owner is Returning: Preliminary Investigations." *Journal of the Society for Psychical Research* 62. 1998. 220-232.

Unexplained Powers of Animals,[4] which showed a dog's awareness of its owner's intentions to come home despite the large distance between them. Dogs, known to be much more sensitive and hyperaware than humans, can pick up on the energy waves sent by their owners from a great distance, affecting their behavior and giving them insight about the owner's actions at the precise time the owner makes a decision. The same is true for humans.

Dr. Rollin McCraty and his colleagues found in their study "The Electricity of Touch: Detection and Measurement of Cardiac Energy Exchange Between People,"[5] that the human heart generates its own powerful electromagnetic field which can actually be detected at least a few feet away by another individual who picks up on the energies emitted from this field.

As a highly intuitive empath myself, I do not subscribe to some of the more skeptical and dismissive

---

[4] Sheldrake, Rupert. *Dogs That Know Their Owners Are Coming Home: And Other Unexplained Powers of Animals*. Three Rivers Press. 2000.
[5] McCraty, Rollin Ph.D., Mike Atkinson, Dana Tomasino, B.A., and William A. Tiller, Ph.D. "The Electricity of Touch: Detection and Measurement of Cardiac Energy Exchange Between People." Karl H. Pribram, ed. *Brain and Values: Is a Biological Science of Values Possible*. Lawrence Erlbaum Associates. Mahwah, NJ. 1998. 359-379.

theories on empathic abilities, but rather cannot help but see the validity in science's newer understandings of emotions of the mind and heart. My opinion, based on my personal research as well as experiences throughout my life and my awareness of how the emotional energies of others affects me, is that everything in life is energy and emits waves of energy which comingle and affect everything around it. Empathic INFJs are highly sensitive to these energy waves, leaving them feeling the effects more strongly than less empathic or non-empathic individuals.

The only way to know how far your empathic abilities extend is to pay close attention to yourself, your feelings, both physical and emotional, and work on becoming in-tune with everything that enters your body. This is a difficult task that can take years or even a lifetime to master. Begin with taking the quick quiz in Table I. This will be the first of many steps in discovering your level of empathic abilities.

When you combine empathic abilities with an INFJ personality type, it can be even more difficult to decipher the constant and intense stream of emotions within yourself. But with the help of the information in this book, using the tools supplied in *The Empathic INFJ Workbook*, as well as focusing on yourself and learning to tune into your body, it is possible to not only fully understand your INFJ empathic abilities, but also to control them and feel like they are working for you rather than against you.

Throughout this book I will be discussing the emotional and physical aspects of an empath which manifest in day to day living. You will often see me referring to these forces as energies, in waves as well as surrounding fields, which contain both emotional and physical symptoms and information.

ARE YOU AN EMPATH?   Table I.

Do you find public or crowded places overwhelming and draining?	Y or N
Do you feel a strong level of empathy towards those around you, regardless of their personal situation?	Y or N
Do you sometimes know information about others without them needing to tell you?	Y or N
Does your mood sometimes change dramatically without any clear cause or trigger?	Y or N
Do you suffer from unexplained physical ailments that may come and go randomly?	Y or N
Are troubled individuals attracted to you, unloading their problems on you without any prompting?	Y or N
Do you find yourself frequently fatigued, despite decent sleeping patterns and overall positive health?	Y or N
Does your mood change upon entering a new location (i.e. indoors, outdoors, work, home, etc.)?	Y or N
Do you randomly think of or feel the emotions of a loved one living far away?	Y or N
Have you been diagnosed with a personality disorder (i.e. Schizophrenia, Borderline Personality Disorder, or Bipolar Disorder)?	Y or N

ARE ALL INFJS EMPATHS?

The terms intuitive and empathic have become synonymous for some, causing confusion about what each actually means. It is incredibly important to note the difference before proceeding with the discussion of whether or not all INFJs are empaths.

Intuitive, as the name suggests, is looking inside of oneself. It is turning into your own person to retrieve knowledge that allows you to make a more accurate judgment. This can be personal knowledge or the collective knowledge Carl Jung often discussed in his works. Intuition is the subconscious mind accumulating and processing external information without conscious awareness. Intuitives pick up a great deal of subtle information during their daily experiences and this information is then processed and stored without conscious awareness. This information is then brought to the conscious part of our brain giving us the feeling that we "just know" something without being aware of the source of this knowledge. Intuition, then, is the ability to look inside ourselves for information that we have gathered. It involves the transferring of this information from the subconscious to the conscious, using mainly the mind.

Empath, however, is exact the opposite of intuition. Empathic abilities have nothing to do with what is on the inside of an individual, nor does it refer to any knowledge or hyperawareness of a situation. Rather, to be an empath refers to how we relate to external forces, or energies, which exist all around us as waves and auras, leaving empaths able to absorb them.

Simply put, intuition is all about looking inside oneself to seek knowledge or understanding based on experiences and subconscious awareness. Empathic abilities are picking up things from outside of ourselves.

With this clearer distinction, we can now come back to the question of whether or not all INFJs are empaths. We know that all INFJs are intuitive, of course, even if the levels of intuitive abilities vary from one person to the next. However, there is no way to possibly state whether or not all INFJs are empaths. Nothing about the description of an intuitive in either Jung's or Myers' and Briggs' works definitively states an ingrained empathic ability. The Myers-Briggs typology is based entirely on how the brain functions by receiving and processing information. This gives no indication of how one would be affected by energy waves and frequencies around them.

Unfortunately, there is no conclusive way to determine whether all INFJs could be empaths, but it would be safer to assume that this is not the case unless or until further evidence linking them arises. My personal experience with those who state they are INFJs has shown a shocking lack of understanding about empathic abilities leaving me to believe that, just as all empaths are not INFJs, all INFJs are not necessarily empaths.

With this reasoning, if you are an INFJ, take special note in reading this book. If these concepts do not speak to or apply to your personal experiences, this may indicate that, despite being an INFJ, you may not be an empath.

NATURE VS. NURTURE

Just as we are unsure of the science behind what makes a person an empath, there is also a great deal of uncertainty about why someone becomes an empath. There are numerous theories, ranging from nurture-based to nature-based or a combination of the two.

Some believe that everyone is born an empath and, long before our modern day hustle and bustle lifestyle which separates us from the nature with which we were created to work in-tune, that each individual had the ability to pick up on and understand all the energies that exist around us. It is with our lifestyle choices that we become less aware and less sensitive, leading some to stray from their natural born instincts.

Others think that being an empath is more likened to a psychological disorder. With a large number of empaths reporting traumatic and abusive pasts, it is thought that the empathic traits are in fact coping mechanisms created by an abused mind, altering the brain chemistry just as in Post-Traumatic Stress

Disorder, Schizophrenia, or any other host of mental disorders.

There are those that subscribe to the idea that empathic traits are actually inherited just like the color of one's hair or an athletic ability.

Some even go so far as to claim religious or spiritual purposes given directly from the Divine. Empaths are here as prophets or seers to correct others and guide them on their paths toward the heavens.

All of these and many more theories are well worth considering when we ponder our own empathic abilities. There may not be one correct answer, as each person's life and personal formation is unique, but looking at our own past in an attempt to discover why we are the way we are can offer some insights about our gifts.

Looking for the reason why, though important in consideration, should not be the main focus of one on their journey to learning about and accepting themselves. Regardless of the reasons we may feel differently and experience the world unlike those around us, the simple truth is that we do. It is important to not look at ourselves as broken or in need of fixing. Our pasts, through genetics, ancestral roots, life experiences or any other hosts of theories, have made us who we are today. The only way to fully understand ourselves is through releasing all the personal and external judgments of those who do not understand and are merely searching for reasons and labels in order to justify a unique existence. You require no justification, only acceptance and understanding.

Whether the cause of empath is nature, nurture or a combination of the two, we each have our own level of empathic abilities based on our own individualities.

LEVELS OF EMPATHIC ABILITIES

The term empath, even when accurately defined, is a fairly broad term. While we can agree on the basic definition of being able to feel what another feels, to what degree is not encompassed within the term. Each individual has a unique level of empathic abilities that only they themselves can accurately measure. Some find they have very little, if any, empathic abilities yet can feel general sympathy towards another person. Others have such a high level of abilities that they can lose themselves completely in someone else's situation.

Just like all human traits, empathic abilities should not be a contest. They should not be measured in terms of better or worse. Whether or not having these abilities is a positive thing to be proud of or a frustrating burden will vary depending on the individual and how they use their abilities. By saying one has no empathic abilities, this does not inherently make them "lucky," nor does it make them "less gifted." It just makes them different. The same goes for someone who has a very strong level of empathy. They are not better than others nor are they insane. They just have a different trait. Only by recognizing empathic abilities as a human characteristic that is neither better nor worse than any other characteristic can we accurately look into ourselves to decide where our abilities lie on the spectrum.

It is important to be honest with oneself when considering your empathic abilities. To tell yourself that you have a high level just because you would like to will do you no good in the long run. To lie to yourself and say you have little to no empathic ability when in fact you are very keen on the emotions of others will only cheat you out of an opportunity to improve your life and hone your skill for more positive purposes. Every person has the capacity to improve their level of empathy or better control an already high aptitude. Learning your base point by being completely honest and genuine with yourself is the most important first step toward taking the path you choose to get where you would like to be as an empath.

To begin considering what it means to have empathic abilities, allow me to give you an analogy that you can easily call to mind when you are curious about your feelings and the feelings of others in any given situation. Imagine that everyone is born with a lens. Each person's lens differs in both thickness and scope. The thickness of the lens determines your level of empathic abilities and the scope of your lens determines how broadly these abilities apply.

Imagine an individual standing in the middle of a crowded room talking to a friend. If this individual has very little empathic ability and is generally unaware of the milieu of people around them, but rather can effortlessly stay focused on the friend they are conversing with, then they would have a thick, zoomed lens. If, however, they had strong empathic abilities that are causing them to absorb emotions of many of the other people in the room, they have a thin, panoramic lens. It may also be possible that this individual has some empathic abilities yet only seems to absorb the emotions of the friend directly in front of them. In this case, their lens would be thin with a focused zoom.

While the two major extremes exist, most people fall somewhere in the middle with varying degrees of lens thickness and zoom capabilities. No one's lens size or width is set in stone and they can vary depending on several factors, such as level of exhaustion, comfort, type of energies of the people around them, dietary changes or, for the more advanced empaths, choice.

To learn what your lens looks like, consider how you feel in certain situations. Ask yourself the following questions:

- Are you overwhelmed by large groups of people?
- Do you lose focus on one person amidst a crowd?
- Does your mind often wander or do you feel fog or fatigue when trying to focus in a busy location?

27

If you answered yes to these questions, odds are your lens scope tends to me more open, absorbing information on a larger scale. If you answered no, then you have a more focused zoom, allowing you to better control your energetic input.

Now consider these questions:

- Is it difficult for you to tell how those around you feel?
- Do you find yourself confused or caught off guard by the emotional responses of people around you?
- Can you easily understand the source of your emotions?

If you answered yes to the questions above, then you probably have a thicker lens, blocking a lot of the emotional energy that others naturally give off. However, if you answered no, you have a thinner lens, allowing in more energetic data.

Once you have a better understanding of your empathic abilities, you can decide where you wish to change, improve or enhance your gifts. Take a moment to write down where you think you are currently at (thin and focused, thick and focused, thin and panoramic, etc.). Below that, jot down where you wish to be, whether a specific consistency or just having more control.

Perhaps your lens is very thick and focused and you wish you were more able to pick up on the emotions of others. If this is the case, then I recommend seeking out resources to hone in on your empathy level. Feel free to continue reading, but this book may not be right for you.

If, however, you find your lens is on the thinner side and set to panoramic view, then you may be interested in learning how to better control your lens, allowing you to concentrate more or thickening your lens when things become overwhelming. If that is the case, this book may be able to help you better control your zoom and focus.

As you read, remember that each person's level of empathic abilities is different. Some people have gifts that many would consider psychic and others cannot understand. To be one of these individuals can be frightening and confusing. It is important to note that this book is intended to help any empathic INFJ who is struggling with how to cope with their abilities no matter where their lens may fall on the spectrum of thickness.

As you read, decide whether or not the information applies to you. If it does not, then consider that it may apply to another reader. We are all individuals with our own journeys and each of us is on a different place in our path.

THRIVING AS AN
EMPATHIC INFJ

KNOW YOURSELF

One of the greatest struggles of an empathic INFJ is figuring out what energy belongs to them, and what belongs to someone else. Lines can easily become blurred when energies and emotions are shared. An empath can be completely sure of themselves and how they feel, but upon taking one step out their front door and seeing another person or even flipping on the news or opening their social media page, all of their self-assuredness is tossed into personal turmoil. They go from standing on solid ground to wading through a desert of quicksand. Emotions become difficult to peg, let alone work through, causing opinions to flutter and waver, leaving the once sure INFJ now a puddle of confusion and self-doubt.

Some empaths struggle so desperately in this sea of lost self that they begin to question their mental health and are often labeled by professionals as having Borderline Personality Disorder or Dissociative (Multiple) Personality Disorder, which only worsens their problem. When diagnosed with such disorders, the empath is left believing that the emotions they are feeling are completely of their own creation and that their lack of ability to hold onto their self is, in actuality, a personal failure as opposed to revealing the truth of what is happening and giving them tools to control it, in turn finding themselves and shaking off any self-doubt or confidence crushing labels.

The truth is, these empaths are not struggling with personality disorders, nor are they incapable of having and holding onto a sense of who they are. They are merely lacking the understanding of what is occurring. Once they have that understanding, they can pause, regroup, reconnect with themselves and continue forward. This takes more than just knowledge. With learning what is happening, the empath also must put forth an ample amount of practice, continued understanding and take complete responsibility for themselves and their feelings. A difficult road, indeed, but a very possible and rewarding one.

In order to be able to hold onto your sense of self no matter whom you may encounter, you must know who you actually are. Many people can grow up never truly connecting with the truth inside of them. We live in a society that rewards conformity, from school life to career and family choices. Mainstream is the only stream where many people feel safe, even if that means abandoning or never actually knowing who they truly are.

As an empath, this is even more prominent. Growing up, while others are learning what they like and do not like, what they stand for or what they stand against, and what defines themselves as individuals, the empath is often struggling through a foreign and lonely land that no other understands, making them frightened and isolated at best, depressed and suicidal at worst.

The empathic INFJ gets tossed around by others as a confidant and impromptu therapist, leaving them busy dealing with the growth of their friends and loved ones. When this is not occurring, they are still very focused on the energies and emotions of those around them, fraught with processing it and wondering why they feel the emotions they are feeling when they cannot understand the sources.

How is it possible to learn yourself when you are too busy focusing on those around you? Even if you have a chance to focus on yourself, the data that you assess when looking into your mind and feelings is so overwhelming, confusing and unexplainable that sorting through it without the knowledge of your gifts is asking quite a lot from a developing youth.

And so, the empath stuffs down a lot of the emotions they cannot understand, wonders why they struggle when everyone around them seems to be figuring themselves out, and ultimately shifts to self-destructive thinking that something must be wrong with them or they must be broken. They enter adulthood with no true identity since the only identity that makes sense is never a solution to be offered.

Here, I wish to offer you that solution; a solution that will show you that you are not broken. You are not disordered. You are not incapable of self-identity. Above all, you do not have to run from the confusion of your mind any longer. You can shine light on that which was misunderstood by you and those around you and dance in the rainbow of your abilities.

WHO ARE YOU?

Whether or not you believe you know who you are, if you are uncertain about your opinions or feeling as though you have no personal boundaries, and especially if you have been diagnosed with a personality disorder, odds are, you do not truly know yourself. And that is okay. You can learn yourself. Just like meeting a new friend, you can have many conversations with yourself, tossing around ideas and opinions, and get to know who you truly are, inside and out.

This is not an overnight practice. It takes years to understand who you are, especially since life causes you to feel as though you are constantly changing. The key to staying familiar in your relationship with yourself is the same as any relationship. You must nourish it daily, revisit it often and commit in love to sticking by your side through good times and bad. By doing this, you can learn who you are, which not only puts you light-years ahead of many in our current society, but will make you recognize your empathic abilities as a positive trait and help you use your skills rather than feel used by them.

If you have learned that you are an INFJ, then you have taken a very important first step that can help you on your journey to self-discovery. Take that understanding and learn as much as you can about your personality type. Researching how you brain works will help you realize that you are not broken. Your mind works just fine. It just works differently than you were taught it was supposed to, and that is okay. You are not alone.

Through your research, it is vital that you absorb the information and put it through a personal filter. By this I mean not to let the information shape you, but rather to assess each new piece of knowledge and decide whether or not it fits you. Learning about yourself only works if you do not allow the research to box you in. There is a lot of information out there about what it means to be an INFJ but that does not mean it will all apply to you. Every person is different. Labels are there to help us understand and launch ourselves to be better, not to hinder our growth and keep us boxed in and stagnant.

Think of yourself as a table. You and those around you have given yourself the label of a table. You have four legs and a flat surface. You are made of nails and wood. There is no doubt in your mind that you are a table. The essence of who you are becomes defined in that simple word: table. But that does not define your limits; it only tells you what you are so that you can feel confident in having an understanding of self. Now you can decide what table you want to be. A formal dining table? A casual breakfast nook table? An office table? A table saw? By learning your initial label, the label that fit and made you feel safe and comfortable, you could build your confidence and research all there was to know about what it means to be that label. But that never means you are harnessed by or entirely defined by what you read about the label. Nothing will ever completely define you, nor should it. You define you, but that label gives you a safe launching point, describing you just enough to make exploring a little further seem less scary.

As you continue to learn more about yourself, each piece of self-discovery becomes comfortable letting you move a little further in your personal exploration.

It is like building a pier over a lake. To go from standing on the shore to plummeting into the center of the lake sounds terrifying. You have no clue how to get out there and even if you did, what would you do out in the middle of the water? Instead, you begin to build one piece at a time. You place the boards down to create a solid, safe foundation so that you are able to confidently reach out another step. You can explore each space before staking the next post or laying the next board, knowing that where you stand is safe. Learning your label is standing on the shore and each piece that you research is taking you out another board until you get into the depth of understanding that rests in the center.

In order to learn who you are, you must research. Start with what you know and read all you can. Learn your personality type. Are you an introvert or ambivert? Do you have a strong introverted thinking function or do you lean heavily on extroverted feeling? Learn your love language.[6] Is it gift giving or acts of service? Words of affirmation, physical touch or quality time? Discern your strongest learning style, whether auditory, kinesthetic, or visual. Learn your favorite color and consider why. Your favorite music. The type of taste you prefer in cuisines. Preferred book genre. Learn *you*.

To learn who you are when you are alone is the best way to understand who you are when you are with other people. It makes the boundaries more clear and makes foreign energies and emotions easier to detect. If you know when you are by yourself how you feel about kittens, then you will know that any differing emotions you suddenly feel towards kittens do not actually belong to you.

CHECK IN WITH YOURSELF

Checking in with yourself is incredibly important in learning who you are. Reading and researching brings with it a great amount of assistance, but unless you can

---

[6] Chapman, Gary. *The Five Love Languages: How to Express Heartfelt Commitment to Your Mate.* Northfield Publishing. 2004.

look into yourself, then the input will not help you much. The best way to do this is to check in with yourself purposefully a few times a day, more at the beginning of learning this exercise.

To check in with yourself, simply take a moment in any situation and ask yourself a few questions:

What emotions am I experiencing right now? Describe in detail how you are feeling, even if you are unsure whether the feelings belong to you or not. Do you feel happy? Frustrated? Content? Confused? Any anxiety or anger? Sadness or depression? It is possible to feel contradictory emotions at once, so do not discount any that you think are in conflict.

Do not just recognize the feeling, but actively give it a name or a label. At this time, you are not giving any assessment of why you feel the way you do or whether or not you should. No berating or self-judgment. Simply recognize how you are feeling and label it.

What sensory input do I recognize right now? This is more about focusing on the senses which can be a difficult and easy-to-dismiss task for many INFJs whose extroverted sensing function is the least developed consciously.

Consider your comfort level. Are you hot or cold? Any pain, soreness or headaches? What about the things you are touching or are touching you, like clothing, a chair or a pet. Is it rough? Smooth? Soft? Pleasant? Force yourself to be present with your senses. What do you smell, taste, or hear? Label it and be aware of it.

What do I want? After checking in with how you feel and forcing yourself to become present in the moment through your sensory input, ask yourself what it is that you want in that moment. It can be something as simple as wanting a bagel or as complex as a major career change. But it is important to only focus on what you want. Not what the people around you want or need. Not what others may think of your answer. There are no right or wrong answers here. Just remember to be honest and withhold judgment. You are allowed to be selfish in your answer.

By taking a couple of minutes several times a day to ask yourself these three questions, you will be more able to learn who you are apart from the events happening around you. This exercise can take some practice and may be difficult to remember in busier situations. But it is often in those hectic moments that this practice is best served.

Consider setting an alarm on your phone or watch to remind you periodically throughout the day. There are some great task trackers and motivational apps on smartphones today that alert you at random intervals to remind you of something you should be thinking about. If you know you are going to be in a large group of people at a busy event or have a chaotic schedule of meetings at work, be deliberate about scheduling a notification in the heat of one of these moments as well as during solitary down time.

The more often you ask yourself these questions and check in, the easier it will be to remember and eventually, after a few weeks or months, it will be second nature to be aware of your feelings and wants.

WHAT EMOTIONS ARE YOURS?

Once you are more aware of yourself in any given situation, it will be easier to look at those feelings and recognize what belongs to you and what you have picked up from those around you. Some emotions and energies will be more obvious to pinpoint as belonging to someone else than others. There are empathic INFJs who are very well-developed in their abilities that can still be caught off guard by certain energies that come their way.

It is important to note that we are always responsible for our own emotions, just like everyone else. While empaths have the ability to pick up on the emotions of others and those emotions can dramatically influence and affect our own emotions, we must still take responsibility for how we feel in any given circumstance. Using the emotions of others as an excuse for our feelings or behaviors is not a sign of maturity or emotional health.

On the same note, other people should not be given the ability or responsibility to control or dictate our emotions. Though it may not feel like it when you experience someone else's emotions, their emotions are always theirs and yours are always your own.

With that said empaths will still absorb the emotions of others and it is necessary to learn to recognize which emotions belong to you and the source of the alien ones so that you can better account for the energies that are in your space and affecting your responses.

Checking in with your emotions often as stated before is the first step. When you do this frequently enough, you will begin to stay actively aware of how you feel, making it easier to spot any sudden changes, whether physically or emotionally, in your body.

If you have been checking in with yourself all day and feeling overall well, content and calm and suddenly you sense anger or a mild headache, you can recognize the new feeling and decide its origin. Perhaps someone just cut you off in traffic, making the spike in anger clearly your own. Or maybe you had an extra cup of coffee at lunch, leaving you with a lingering headache. But if you ponder this new information and cannot find a source, odds are the emotion or feeling does not belong to you.

Depending on your situation, say being surrounded by familiar coworkers, family or friends, you can ask around to see if anyone is experiencing any anger or headaches. More often than not, you will find the source amongst you. If, however, you are not able to query those around you, it may be safe to assume that you are picking up on someone else's energy if you cannot pinpoint a personal cause.

Continue checking in with your feelings frequently over the couple of hours following the change and see how things progress. You may notice that the feeling fades away as the source distances, further confirming that the feelings were not your own. On the other hand, if the anger builds or the headache worsens and you still cannot see a reason why you would be experiencing these feelings, try leaving the situation, seeking solitude if possible, to attempt to diminish these foreign energies.

Energies and emotions that do not belong to you tend to follow a few common signs which are important to note upon checking in with yourself throughout the day and noticing your feelings. These include:

- **Sudden onset**. Usually feelings, both physical and emotional, do not pop up out of the blue. If you experience a sudden change in how you feel without an obvious cause, it may be a sign that the feeling is being picked up from someone else.

- **Very weak or very strong**. When picking up other people's energies, they tend to manifest in our bodies as very weak, almost difficult to detect, or blaringly strong. Most adults feel day to day moods on a fairly temperate scale, short of obvious instances of elation, surprise or anger, so if a feeling seems to be mildly hovering in the distance, you may be catching glimpses of someone else's moderate temperament. If the feeling is over-the-top strong with no clear purpose, then someone close to you is probably experiencing a short episode outside of their normal moderate temperament (or in some instances, they may be emotionally unhealthy and carrying loud frequencies of energies with them wherever they go).

- **Conflicting.** While most emotionally mature adults can handle two conflicting emotions at one time, it is rare that one is not stronger than the other at any given time. If you feel emotions that seem to conflict strongly, almost as though they are competing for your attention, you may be dealing with someone else's emotions.

- **Unfamiliar.** While this one seems obvious, it can actually manifest in a very confusing fashion. Most people, given their lives of ups and downs, have learned how their emotions feel. Anger is familiar as is sadness, joy and contentedness. But each individual feels these emotions in a different way. If you feel an emotion that seems unfamiliar or confusing, one where you may not be able to give it a name, this may be a feeling coming from an outside source. Empaths have the ability to feel exactly what those around them feel, even if that means it is an emotion outside of their normal realm of understanding.

As you go through your daily checks and ask yourself about your emotions and feelings, particularly while you attempt to name each one, consider these points. It may help you wade through what is yours and what is not.

Just as asking yourself how you feel might initially seem awkward and uncomfortable, deciding whether or not the feelings are your own could take you a step further outside of your comfort zone. Most are not taught this practice and thus it can be a little strange, even leading you to question your sanity.

While you consider these aspects of your feelings, try to step back and release all judgment, both of yourself and those around you. Emotions need recognition and validation in order to function properly. Any judgment hinders their process, therefore hindering your ability to deal with them. You need to treat the emotions of others that have entered into your energy with the same gentle care you would treat your own.

DEALING WITH FOREIGN ENERGIES

Now that you have worked to pinpoint which emotions and energies belong to you and which are picked up from friends, family or random passers-by, you are left wondering what to do with these emotions. In some instances, removing yourself from the situation that houses the energy is enough to dissipate the feelings and allow you to regain your sense of balance. But what if you cannot leave the situation? Or what if leaving does not work and you are still carrying around someone else's baggage? There are things you can do in these instances that will help you process and remove these emotions.

Since life can become chaotic and leave us with little time and energy to focus on ourselves, especially in the heat of the moment when we are unable to escape a busy situation, it is always important to have some go-to tricks up your sleeve, or as I say, in your "tool bag." Your tool bag is basically an easy-to-remember resource composed of ideas that can help you in any given situation, without the need to stop and research or learn something new. Everyone's tool bag looks a little different since each person has different methods that will work for them. It is possible to have too much in your tool bag, as it then turns into a decision bag leaving you to recall too much information and then select something when you have bigger things on your mind. For that reason, you should always try on new ideas for handling emotions and energies of others when you are in a comfortable situation that allows you some leisure. This way, you can easily learn what works for you and what does not, allowing you to only fill your tool bag with surefire methods to balance your emotional state.

Your tool bag should never be left to get dusty. As we change, our needs change. For that reason, continuous trial and error as well as ongoing personal research for more tools is a great way to keep you feeling your best and allowing you to adapt to any of life's unexpected situations.

A great way to call to mind your resource list is to make it as sensual as possible. Our brains are hardwired to remember things through our senses, so attaching as many senses as you can to your tool bag will make it easier to call to mind in a pinch. It may sound hokey, but take a moment now to visualize your tool bag. Give it a color, a shape, a size. Does it look like a stylish designer purse? Or perhaps an athletic duffle bag? I like to call to mind a pink tool kit lined with yellow trim to house my resources. Now imagine yourself lifting it. Of course, it should be lightweight since you will be carrying it around with you everywhere you go. Visualize moving it back and forth between your hands and really focus on how the bag feels. Listen for any rustling or jingling of zippers. Next, visualize smelling the bag. Does it smell like plastic straight from the store? What about a favorite cologne?

After you have gone through this exercise, you should have a pretty good sense of what your tool bag is like. Here, I will offer you a few of my favorite solutions for handling the energies of others that I frequently place in my tool bag. As you read each suggestion, visualize yourself placing it inside of your tool bag. Remember that some of these may not work for you, and that's okay. You can easily remove them from your bag and only keep the ones you find beneficial, also adding more of your own later on.

Try not to dismiss any of these techniques until you have put them into action. By doing so, you may be cheating yourself out of the best tool for you. They may seem simple, silly or strange, but each one has its benefits and can help balance your emotional energy allowing you to feel more like you again, and less like a sponge for others.

TOOL BAG

Emotional Freeing Technique. Emotional Freeing Technique (EFT) is a powerful tool used by many therapists today. You may have heard it referred to as "tapping" as the basis of the technique is to tap specific parts of your body which are considered the ends or beginnings of energy channels which flow through our bodies.

If you imagine that the emotions and feelings that we absorb from those around us are energy waves, you can see how they could either flow through our bodies or get stuck. When an empath is feeling less balanced and more overwhelmed, that is a sign that their energy is getting backed up, leaving them vulnerable for more energy to join the blockage.

EFT clears out this blockage. By tapping specific points on your body, it stimulates these energy channels, shaking up the blockage and breaking it apart, allowing the channel to then flow freely. Once this happens, the energies you have picked up from those around you can flow through your system and right out, leaving you feeling free and energized.

Picture your energy channels as a box of cornstarch. There is a small opening for the cornstarch to flow through when tipped over a bowl at the right angle. Once you tilt the box too far, the hole becomes overwhelmed by the amount of cornstarch flowing towards it, ultimately blocking it and ceasing the flow of cornstarch. By simply tapping on the side of the box, it breaks apart the buildup, allowing the cornstarch to once again flow freely out of the opening. Just a couple of taps and things are back on track.

Table II shows you the main tapping points for EFT. They begin on the top of your head and work all the way down to your fingertips. Each spot only needs to be tapped around seven or eight times to be effective, but there is no limit to the number of rounds of tapping you can do. If after the first round you still feel lingering emotions of others, go ahead and start again. After each time through, check in with your emotions. Pinpoint what you feel and decide again whether or not the feelings belong to you. After a few rounds of EFT, if you still feel the same emotions at the same level of strength as before you started, consider that they may be your own or that you may need to work on processing them a little further.

To go through the entire tapping technique certainly would look strange if done in front of others. For this reason, I recommend slipping away to a bathroom or heading out to your car if you are in a public place. In a case where the situation does not allow you to leave, there is a milder alternative that can help you clear up some of the energy blockage without leaving your friends phoning the men in white coats.

Refer again to the image in Table II. Note point "G" on the collarbone and point "L" on the side of the hand. These are two points that many people touch subconsciously when they are stressed, overwhelmed or in need of comfort as our subconscious know what our bodies need to bring balance. It is not uncommon to see people tapping or rubbing these spots in everyday life. When you are in a public space and need to discreetly work out your energies through EFT, gently tap point "G" and rub point "L" until you notice an improvement. Those around you probably will not even notice the slight movement and those who do will see it as natural, having subconsciously done the same in the past. Then

Table II. Emotional Freeing Technique Tapping Points

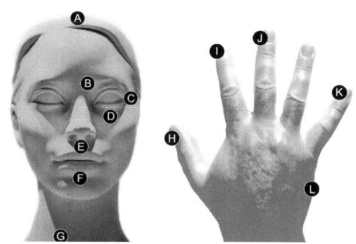

Tap each point seven times:

- A. Directly on the center of your crown.
- B. On the brow bone at the beginning of your eyebrow.
- C. At the corner of the eye, on the eye socket bone.
- D. Below your eye, on the eye socket bone.
- E. Directly below your nose.
- F. On the indent below your lip and above your chin.
- G. On the out-jutting ball of your collar bone.
- H. On the edge of your thumbnail.
- I. On the edge of your index fingernail.
- J. On the edge of your middle fingernail.
- K. On the edge of your pinky fingernail.
- L. On the side of your hand, "karate chop" point.

when you can seek some solitude, run through all the points if you still feel weighed down by the energies of others.

Emotional Processing. As I mentioned earlier, when we experience any emotions, it is important to recognize them and accept them in order to process them. This applies to the emotions that do not necessarily belong to us as well. When doing your check in, you have recognized the emotion, so the next step to removing it is allowing yourself to process it. Sometimes this can be quick and painless, especially if they are easier, low key emotions, but others may take a little more time.

If you pick up joyful and excited emotions, those would be easy to allow yourself to feel. Consider it like a free boost and ride the high. No harm can come from you enjoying the joy of others, even if you are not particularly feeling joyful yourself.

The more difficult emotions can be those of anger, sorrow or fear. No one likes to experience these emotions and it can feel unfair that empaths are burdened with the extra dose of processing someone else's pain, but accepting that it is part of our makeup will help make the situation easier. It is difficult enough handling the negative energies so there is no sense adding self-pity or personal anguish and loathing to the mix.

Instead, feel it. Feel the sadness as though it were your own. Breathe through the anger. Confront the fear. Emotions will not hurt you. They are just feelings that only have as much control as you allow them. You are always in charge of them, even when it feels like you are not, so take charge and confront them just as you should with your personal moods.

Once the emotions have been approached and felt, they tend to slip away. They are like a needy puppy that just wants you to notice it and give it a little pat. After you tend to them, they will move on and find something else to do. So accept the emotion, allow it, feel it and be done with it.

Energy Field Cleansing Meditation. This technique may take a little time getting comfortable and familiar with, but once you master it, it will almost feel second nature and can be used in any situation with ease. It is a simple visualization exercise that focuses the mind and allows you to feel in control of your body, your energy field and what you allow in it.

Picture those around you as having a force field surrounding their bodies. Call it whatever you prefer: an energy field, aura, emotional excess or any other term you feel comfortable with. Give this field a color if that helps you picture it. Each person can have the same color or different colors. You can visualize the field as a cloud surrounding the person, or perhaps it has more water-like appearance flowing around the body. Maybe it is a light glowing around them. See this field as an attachment to their body; something that seems sewn on and held closely in. It looks tailored and conformed, almost like a nice-fitting garment, not jumping out toward you or anyone else. Their field stays close to them.

Now visualize the same thing around yourself. See it moving, as water, fog or light. Notice how yours does not fit like everyone else's. Rather than being controlled and held tightly to your body, your field seems to hang loosely, flapping in the breeze, going wherever it pleases. See it being pulled toward those around you like a magnet to metal. Watch as it reaches out, intermingles with the fields of those around you, flowing toward them like a river. Now watch it as it comes back to you. Notice the pieces of the other person's field floating in it, washing back towards your body, stuck like fish in a neat or flies on a spider's web. This stuff remains in your field, just hanging there, as it continues to dance around and pull in more and more energies from the fields of those nearest you.

Now imagine that you can control your field. It is fully under your power. Reach out and grab it, reel it in, pulling it close to your body as you would a blanket on a cold winter evening. Pull it away from those around you and bring it completely back to yourself. Harness it. Sew it back onto your body and do not allow it to flow freely away any longer. If it feels like it wants to linger, firmly tell it no. Visualize it staying on you and only you.

But you will see that it is still full of all that other stuff it pulled in from those around you. Visualize shaking it out like dust off an old rug. Watch as the energies that are not yours fall to the ground below you. Envision pure, crisp water flowing through your field, washing out whatever remains, cleansing it of any energy that does not belong to you. See your field going from muddled and cloudy to pure and free. Watch as it glistens and shines, empty of all that is not yours. Feel how lightweight it is as you wear it. How much easier it is to carry around, controlled and free of baggage.

Any time you feel like your field wants to move toward another, remind yourself that no good comes from pulling in unwanted energies. Absorbing the energy of those around you does not lessen their burdens or struggles. It only adds to yours, clouding up and weighing down your field, leaving you less capable of offering the assistance they may truly need.

It takes mindfulness and practice to master this meditation. You will need to spend some time meditating on it, creating a visual that you can easily call to mind in the midst of an overwhelming crowd, but overtime you will be able to harness your field, keeping it in and cleaning and emptying it when it manages to wiggle out again.

Believe that you can control what comes into your emotional space and you will control it.

Earthing or Grounding. When we look at the emotions and feelings that we absorb from others as actual substances rather than just ideas or concepts, we recognize how they can become trapped inside of ourselves. While things like exercise, mindfulness and even Emotional Freeing Techniques can greatly improve the flow of these energies, allowing them to work their way out of our bodies, it stands to reason that they will linger around us if they have nowhere to go.

Everything around us works on a frequency and what our frequency is dictates what we attract and what we can put out. By keeping our body on the frequency it was created for, we can stay balanced and energies of others easily flow in and out, without remaining stagnant and throwing off our natural rhythm.

The best way to restore our natural frequency is through Earthing, or some may call it Grounding. This is the simple act of touching the earth. By doing so, we can give the energies an outlet into the soil while we absorb the energies we were intended from the earth. Simply removing your shoes, lined with rubber soles that prevent the transfer of energy, our feet become portals for all the energy built up within us from other individuals and objects, sending it right back to where it belongs, freeing us.

While it does require you to be outside, this method works on almost any surface from sand and dirt to concrete and brick, as long as it is in direct contact with the ground and not inhibited by any external influences, especially rubber or metal. Shoot to touch the earth at least once a day for an hour to balance yourself and release built up energy. The more you touch the earth, the better you will naturally feel, regardless of your emotional situation. It will re-center you and bring you back to balanced.

Cleansing Bath. As we go through our daily activities, we are surrounded by energies of all types which can basically cling like dirt to an empath. A cleansing bath is a great way to detoxify ourselves of these foreign energies and bring balance to ourselves. The best ingredients for an energy cleansing bath are Epsom salt and sage. Epsom salt is known to draw out the physical aspects of the negativity in our bodies, acting as a detoxifying agent. Sprinkle one cup of the salts into warm bath water and soak for at least twenty minutes.

Sage has been used for centuries in many practices to rid spaces of negativity energy. While some believe sage possess certain qualities that can cleanse negative energy, others feel it is just a means of focusing your mind on what you wish to happen which, in turn, creates thoughts which force out any unwanted energy. Either way, many religions and belief structures practice some form of cleansing with sage.

Smudging, which is the act of burning sage and using the smoke to cleanse a room, object or person, is the most common use of sage for this purpose. However, it works in a more concentrated fashion on the body when fully submerged with water. Simply take a couple bundles of dried sage, wrap them in a cloth and steep them in a pot of boiling water just like a tea. Add the water to your Epsom salt bath before you bathe.

Chakra Balancing. Just like EFT channels, our chakras are locations in our body that allow energy to flow freely through. Chakra is Sanskrit for wheel, so envision each chakra as a wheel spinning with the flow of energy, like a water wheel, beginning at our crown and running all the way down to the base of our torso. If these wheels become overwhelmed with energy, they can back up, clogging the free flow and throwing off the body's balance. Since empaths are constantly bombarded with energies, the flow through the chakras must remain open.

Opening blocked chakras should be incorporated into daily practice using exercise, yoga, mantras and diet. For a thorough guide to balancing your chakras, refer to *The Empathic INFJ Workbook* which offers information to determine which chakras are blocked as well as diet, yoga poses and mantras that are easy to learn and apply to any lifestyle.

AVOID OVERWHELMING NEGATIVITY

Empathic INFJs can easily get caught up in the negativity in the world. Sensitive to suffering of any kind, hearing about or witnessing sadness, grief, despair, victimizing or injury leaves the INFJ enveloped with negative emotions that can have a detrimental impact on their life and the lives of those around them.

In a world where information is readily available, even if it is not wanted, it is easy to allow the negativity to run rampant in our minds and encompass our thinking, forcing out the positive and goodwill that exists too. From an angry person we pass on the street to the millions of unjust deaths occurring around the globe, the INFJ is overwhelmed with sadness, frustration and sometimes anger. These feelings can leave the INFJ paralyzed and hopeless, adding to the very negativity of which they wish to eradicate.

Since the empathic INFJ is often an altruistic person incapable of understanding the hatred and cruelty they so often witness, they are left feeling even more alone and separated from the rest of humanity. They find themselves wondering why they are so different. Why do their hearts weigh so heavy? How can they possibly thrive in a world filled with people of such differing values or lack of morals?

With each individual they try to help, each charity they join or lost soul they reach out to, there are so many more who suffer. The INFJ's ability to step back and take in the entire picture of humanity can quickly turn into the very thing that leaves them broken. The large, pessimistic canvas of an image they see splayed across the world more than overshadows the tiny deeds of which they feel so merely capable, causing them to wonder, *what is the point? Why should I continue to try when I am only left with hopelessness and despair, bombarded with constant images and stories of negativity and hatred? Why?*

This becomes the INFJ's habitual line of thinking, almost impossible to pull out of with the constant barrage of media. When details become overwhelming in the mind of an INFJ, it is their default to step back and look at the bigger picture. It is within this big picture that they seek solace from the details that overwhelm their intuitive minds and cause anxiety and frustration. So when the big picture is far more frightening than the minutia, they are left with nothing to escape to. There is no reset button in their minds to bring them back to their purpose.

So how does the empathic INFJ cope in such an overwhelmingly negative world? How do they look at the details and the big picture without being lost in a sea of hopelessness that leaves them paralyzed, only to squander the amazing gifts they have to offer?

The easy answer is to fight the natural tendency to step back and see the big picture. It is contrary to how an INFJ usual copes with stress and yet it is the only way to avoid the overwhelming negativity. You will never find peace when you surround yourself with so much outside of your control. The mind that strives for perfection in an imperfect world will only ever be able to see the bumps, wrinkles and tears in the canvas, completely overlooking the art before their eyes.

Instead, hone in on the smallest area possible, whatever that may be at the time. Focus on one good thing. One good person or deed. One good object or action. Focus with all your intensity and see it entirely for what it is. A good and positive thing, filled with beauty and grace. Take a few moments to recognize it and remind yourself that there is good in the world, even if it is only this one thing.

From there, slowly step back, limiting your view and not allowing yourself to zoom out all the way. Look at an entire room or landscape and look for as much good as you can. Smiles on faces, birds chirping peacefully, or the simple awareness of your living, breathing presence in the space. Tap into your senses here and be specific. You are looking for as much good as you can.

Think of your field of view like a microscope, zoomed in as far as possible, looking at only a single, healthy cell. As you adjust the knob to zoom out, take it slowly. Look at how many new cells have come into focus and count the healthy ones. You may notice a diseased cell here or there, but you are not attempting to focus on them. Count the healthy cells. Make sure you have accounted for each one before you zoom out further and assess the next grouping of cells. Continue to look for the healthy cells and allow yourself to smile with each one you notice. Recognize it for its individuality. Soon you will realize how many more healthy cells there are than diseased ones. The further you zoom out, the more you will see that the petri dish before you is overrun with healthy cells, making the diseased almost appear buried in the sea of them.

The more often you find yourself narrowing your focus and recognizing how much positivity there is in the world, the easier it will become to see it all. Overtime, you will learn to hear or see negative things and find the positivity in them, no matter how miniscule. Like Fred Rogers inspiring quote, "When I was a boy and I would see scary things in the news, my mother would say to me, 'Look for the helpers. You will always find people who are helping.'"

Once your focus shifts to seeing only the positive in every situation, each action you take will suddenly have purpose. You will begin to see how the positivity breeds into more and the ripple effect will only grow stronger.

> "When I was a boy and I would see scary things in the news, my mother would say to me, 'Look for the helpers. You will always find people who are helping.'"
> - Fred Rogers -

With seeing these new ripples of positivity emitting from you and everything around you, you will also begin to see how similar you are to everyone else in the world, diminishing your feelings of loneliness and isolation. When you reach out to help another person close to you, looking for the positive in them and the situation, you will start to see the kindred spirit, a human just as yourself, sitting across from you, bringing you closer together. This will strengthen your ability to aide others and bring positivity to their life while in turn bringing a new found camaraderie to yours. Rather than spending your time wallowing in self-pity about how different you are from those around you, you will rejoice in your similarities.

71

EMPATHIC GUILT

A strong piece of what leaves an empath feeling drained despite using all the right techniques and taking good care of themselves is the feeling of being responsible for a large piece of the world around them. When they are hyperaware of the things happening around them, it becomes much more difficult to ignore them. Everything from the tragedies of war spread across television programs to a suffering bird on the side of the road can send an empath into full help mode.

Not only are empaths cognizant that these injustices and woes are occurring, but they also have a dramatic effect on their emotions and physical feelings. Seeing a bird struggle on the side of the road, especially for an animal empath, can leave them physically aching and wanting to bring an end to that pain. Even a toddler crying in the supermarket can feel like the responsibility of an empath because they feel the true, intense emotions of the child and want to help them reconcile these emotions, freeing themselves in the process.

It is because of this deep energetic connection that the empath feels responsible for things that others would hardly notice. Turning a blind eye does nothing for them when they are still left suffering the pains of another even if they can no longer see them.

But the truth is no one person can solve all the aching in the world, no matter how hard they try. This leaves the empath with what I call *empathic guilt*. Empathic guilt is the feeling of wanting to help, knowing the extent of the suffering, and yet our humanity leaves us incapable of fixing the problem and bringing peace to the situation. Empathic INFJs feel as though they have failed the individual, themself and the world.

The empath starts to feel burdened with a gift that shows them so many in need but is paired with a body that cannot accomplish it all. This guilt can turn into self-loathing, wondering if something is wrong with them. Wondering why they lack the capacity to help everyone they wish to help, burning out as they try and wallowing in frustration about these shortcomings. They are left asking why they have the ability to feel it without the ability to fix it.

This empathic guilt, if left unchecked, can be detrimental to an empath. It can send one into a spiral of depression and poor judgment. It can also leave an empath exposed to those who wish to take advantage of that guilt, opening them up to abusive relationships and friendships, furthering the degenerative emotional cycle.

The truth is that empaths are not responsible for nor should they attempt to fix all of the woes to which they are aware. It is simply impossible. The empath has the awesome ability to feel what those around them feel, making them amazing at helping the people they can, but it is incredibly important to recognize one's own limits as human beings and not beat yourself up for those limits.

The empathic INFJ's capacities to help others are phenomenal and should not be diminished. It can be so easy to look at all the areas in which we fall short, to see everything we cannot do and cannot fix, but we also need to take the time to reflect on what we can do and have done. Every small act of making things better counts for something. We may feel deeply the perils of injustice around the world, in humans, animals and plants, but offering a hug to one suffering child or lending a listening ear to a person in need, is enough.

The things you do are enough, no matter how much it may feel like it is not. Your actions and abilities are enough.

You are enough.

When we recognize that we are enough, that even the smallest acts matter, we can begin to let go of some of our empathic guilt that only serves to lessen our capabilities rather than enhance them. Your gifts were not given to you to burden you with a world's worth of struggles. Rather, they were given to you to help those who you are able.

You do not have to turn a blind eye to the suffering, but in order to lessen the empathic guilt, you do need to turn your focus away from what you cannot do and shine the light solely on what you can do. Recite the wisdom of the Serenity Prayer:

> "God, grant me the serenity to accept the things I cannot change, the courage to change the things that I can, and the wisdom to know the difference."

Empathic INFJs are unique and special, but the world does not rest on your shoulders. Each person has their limits and learning yours will lessen your feelings of guilt.

ESTABLISH HEALTHY BOUNDARIES

The only true way to achieve contentment and peace as an empathic INFJ is to learn and apply healthy boundaries to your life. When we struggle with knowing where our emotions end and another's begin, boundaries essentially are a gray area. Most people have natural, obvious boundaries they can apply to daily life. Even if they struggle in areas of guilt or enabling, certain boundaries are still clear because they are their own person with their own thoughts, bodies and emotions.

Empathic INFJs, on the other hand, do not naturally have these basic boundaries in place because our thoughts, bodies and emotions do not always feel like our own. How can we draw firm boundary lines when the basic black and white areas appear so gray?

The first step is assigning ownership. This part can be difficult when we really are not sure whose feelings and energies are whose. For this reason, being mindful and practicing the techniques described in the "Know Yourself" section of this book are essential to beginning to draw your boundaries. Though it can be easy to feel as though your mind, emotions and sometimes body do not belong only to yourself because it can be affected involuntarily by external elements, it is essential that you recognize and believe that this is not the case. If you feel like your body and energies are not your own, then they never will be.

The first boundary you must draw is establishing that your mind, your body, your emotions and your energies are completely yours. They are controlled by you and only within your power. While you may not feel this is accurate, you have to start here in order to make any progress. Even if you do not currently believe it is possible to have complete ownership over yourself with all the overwhelming external forces affecting you, this is a case of fake it until you make it. Turn it into a daily mantra if it helps.

My body, my mind, my emotions and my energies belong only to me.

Say it over and over again. This boundary line is essential to creating the firm boundaries necessary to live a functional and healthy empathic life.

After you have taken control and recognized full ownership of yourself on top of being mindful of how you feel, you can start setting more concrete boundaries in your day to day life which will further enable you to feel in control and establish yourself as an individual as opposed to someone who gets tossed around by the energies of others.

WHAT ARE BOUNDARIES?

Boundaries come in two different forms: physical boundaries and emotional boundaries. Many people are familiar with physical boundaries. Even most empaths are aware of their personal physical boundaries. These can be recognized in what you allow to touch you or affect your body. Your skin is a very concrete version of a physical boundary. You know that everything on or encased inside of your skin is yours in the physical sense. A doctor cannot choose to operate on you and remove a kidney without your permission. A stranger cannot approach you and grab your body without your permission. Your physical body is yours.

Another version of a physical boundary is property lines. Your home is your own. Your neighbor is not allowed to enter your home whenever they please. The police need a warrant. A burglar is a trespasser. No one can build on your property without your consent. They cannot walk up to your house and pick your flowers. The physical boundaries of your home are clear. As are the physical boundaries of your property, even when not at your home, like your vehicle, purse or wallet, or even your pet.

Empaths, unless other emotional problems are present, are all fairly familiar with and capable of holding firm their physical boundaries. Emotional boundaries, however, are far more complex and difficult to recognize and enforce. These boundaries are very personal to each individual, making them more difficult to understand. Think of the boundary of personal space. There is no wall that shows another person how close they can comfortably come to you, but you feel a certain level of discomfort when they have broached your personal space, regardless of their intention. A spouse or loved one is granted more freedom to broach your space, whereas a complete stranger may have less room before you begin to feel violated.

Emotional boundaries also refer to what you will tolerate as treatment by others. If a coworker tells you to drop your business project to help them with theirs, you may feel violated by their dictation of your time. A verbally abusive friend who badgers you with repeated phone calls may leave you feeling harassed. Your teenage child guilting you into cleaning their room or doing their homework when you had other plans could leave your boundaries feeling trampled.

Many adults understand emotional boundaries simply by listening to their feelings and drawing limits on their time, tasks and emotions by recognizing that which makes them feel uncomfortable. Healthy boundaries allow you to remain who you are and stay consistent in your emotions and feelings no matter what occurs around you.

Non-empathic individuals feel their own emotions and only their own emotions, making boundaries appear more black and white. Of course I am not saying that every non-empathic person has strong personal boundaries, but rather that they have the ability to recognize uncomfortable or violated feelings as being their own as opposed to wondering if those feelings may actually involve someone else and their boundaries.

Allow me to give you an example. Imagine sitting in a waiting room with two other people. All is quiet as you wait, until one person, we will call him Jeff, starts clicking his pen. He starts with just a click here and a click there, but slowly his fiddling increases and the clicking becomes fairly consistent. You can see the second person, Susan, becoming uncomfortable. Her feelings of irritation, gradually shifting to frustration and building into anger are wafting across the room in energy waves that your empathic being is picking up. Susan's boundaries are definitely being violated and the emotions she is feeling clearly represent that.

Since you are now feeling exactly as Susan is about the incessant clicking of Jeff's pen, you feel as though your boundaries have been violated too. You begin to feel angry and annoyed. But instead of being able to firmly declare that your boundaries have been crossed, you cannot help but wonder if it would have bothered

81

you had it not bothered Susan. Her emotions filled your space, leaving you affected by the energies and unsure of whose boundaries were actually crossed. After the situation is complete, you carry the emotions of crossed boundaries with you without having the ability to determine if they were ever truly violated at all.

This happens to empaths countless times, leaving you feeling unable to set your own personal boundaries, feeling as though your boundary lines ebb and flow depending upon who you are with, essentially leaving you boundary-less.

HOW TO DEFINE YOUR BOUNDARIES

The only way to combat this is to firmly define your personal boundaries and stay present and focused in all situations to ensure they are applied fully and accurately. Initially, when you establish your own boundaries of what you will and will not tolerate, how you will allow others to behave towards you and where your responsibilities lie, you may still find yourself struggling to remember them in the moment of being bombarded with other's emotions and boundaries. For this reason, I strongly encourage you to keep a cheat sheet of the following exercise on you at all times. When you begin to feel as though your boundaries are being crossed, allow yourself to take a personal moment, glance through your cheat sheet to remind yourself of your own strong boundaries, and reassess the situation, determining whether your boundaries have in fact been crossed or if you are just feeling the energies of another's trampled lines. After a while, you will be able to quickly call to mind where you stand, the things that bother you or cross your personal boundary lines and be able to act accordingly, regardless of the energies that may swarm around you.

In order to establish your boundaries, you must take a great deal of time in personal meditation. Of course, it is essential that you begin with checking in with yourself and, using some energy cleansing techniques from your tool bag, ensuring that you are not overwhelmed with the energies of others. This will help you look into yourself, uninterrupted and untainted by external forces.

Before you begin, grab a pen and paper, or open up to page 16 of *The Empathic INFJ Workbook*, and set them beside you (not a laptop or cell phone as those can carry energies that may affect your emotions). Select a comfortable space where you feel free and uninhibited, making sure you are completely alone.

Now close your eyes and consider your ideal social interaction. Maybe select a specific individual to call to mind, a loved one, coworker or acquaintance. Think, in detail, of a conversation you have recently had or wish to have with this person. Allow yourself to speak for them, adding in phrases and actions that you wish to see from them throughout the conversation. These should be things that enhance the conversation, make you feel good about the interaction as well as yourself. Maybe they brush your arm with their hand. Perhaps you want them to use more descriptive wording towards how they feel about you. Even adding a contented smile to their face may be enough to bring the interaction to the optimum level. No matter what you wish to see, make sure you envision the conversation in the most positive light, tweaking anything that makes you feel negative.

After you have spent a few moments meditating on this conversation, open your eyes and reach for your paper and pen. Jot down what you remember wishing would happen in the conversation to make it a positive experience. Try to call to mind even the slightest detail, focusing entirely on the other party. Write down facial expressions, tone of voice, phrases and body gestures that brought positivity to you during the meditation. Do not worry about ordering or organizing for now.

Once you have written as much as you could recall, it is time to close your eyes again. This time, using the same individual as before, think of the exact opposite interaction. Visualize what they could do that would leave you feeling horrible, hopeless, devastated or afraid. Go ahead and allow yourself to cover both realistic traits, like statements they have used in the past or facial expressions that made you feel uneasy, as well as far-fetched behaviors, violence or extreme verbal abuse. If at any time you feel yourself slipping into genuine fear or uneasiness due to the vividity of your imagination or triggers from the past, open your eyes and bring yourself back to the present. Remind yourself that you are safe. This is not an exercise intended to bring up uncontrollable negative emotions, but rather one to bring forward awareness of potential encounters.

After you have completed this portion of the meditation, turn to a new page and write down the behaviors and words you envisioned that brought you negative emotions. Exhaust the list and be as specific as you are able.

Now that you have these two lists, it is time to begin building your boundary list. To do this, draw a line down the center of the page creating two columns. At the top of one column write "What I Will Allow." At the top of the second write "What I Will NOT Allow." Begin at the top of your list of positive interaction traits and write down in the "What I Will Allow" section phrases based on your list. For example, if you envisioned a warm smile on your conversationalist's face, you could write "I will allow inviting and pleasant facial expressions." Perhaps you enjoyed the way they complimented your blouse. In this case, write "I will allow platonic compliments of my wardrobe, hair and non-sexual features." Continue on down your list until you have encompassed all of the traits of your positive interaction.

Next, move to the negative interaction list. Translate these in the same manner. If you pictured the person hurting you in any way, write "I will not allow anyone to bring harm to my body, intended or unintended." Maybe they complimented you in a way that made you feel uncomfortable: "I will not allow comments or compliments, no matter how well-intentioned, of my physique or sexual attributes." Continue on until you have included each of the negative interactions.

Do not skip over anything because it seems too obvious. You want this list to be as complete and exhaustive as possible, including the boundary lines of which you have already mastered.

Once you are finished, look through your lists. These are the written rules of your personal boundaries, unchanging in any situation, regardless of the people involved.

KEEPING PERSONAL BOUNDARIES

While determining your personal boundaries can be done individually, upholding and protecting these boundaries can only be done in the midst of attack. This can take a great deal of practice, especially if you have struggled with boundaries in the past. As mentioned before, it will help you to keep a cheat sheet, if not the exhaustive list, on you at all times to make it easier for you to stay focused in the heat of the moment.

Whenever you begin to feel as though a boundary is being crossed, look at your list, decide whether or not it is your boundary or perhaps the energy of another whose boundaries are being violated. If you establish that someone is, in fact, pushing your personal bounds, it is important to stand up for yourself. This does not need to be rude or mean. Depending on the situation, it may be as simple as stepping away or shifting your body language to inform the other person that they have intruded on you, physically or emotionally. In some instances, be prepared to state, politely but forcefully, that you will not tolerate the way they spoke to or treated you. The more often you stand up for your boundaries, the greater you will build your confidence and self-worth as well as strengthen your boundary lines making future violations easier to recognize and handle.

Remember that the list you carry is an exhaustive list. That means that no one gets a free pass to cross over your boundary lines. A stranger with a snide comment should not go ignored just as a spouse who insults you should not be chocked up to tough love. Your boundaries must remain firm in order for them to strengthen and for you to improve your sense of self. This will require you to combat your sense of empathic guilt in some situations, but it is never selfish to protect your personal boundaries. You help no one by allowing them to be violated.

PART OF THE WORLD

THE WORLD AROUND YOU

Despite how the empathic INFJ may feel at times, it is not very feasible to live in a vacuum. Due to their natural altruistic desire to help those around them, INFJs tend to crave human interaction after a period of comfortable solitude. It is not uncommon for the empathic INFJ to seek this interaction only to quickly become overwhelmed with energies and long to get away, leaving their social quota lacking and their empathic abilities exploding making for an unpleasant and depressing mix.

Fortunately, there are ways to balance the conflicting pieces of your personality without leaving you hopeless and frustrated.

EVERYDAY OUTINGS

Even when you wish to seek solitude, the reality is that life demands certain unavoidable responsibilities which require leaving the comfort of your house walls. Going to work on a regular basis, frequenting grocery stores, stopping by the bank or any multitude of actions that involve either conversing with another individual or being surrounded by unfamiliar people are a necessity, and a healthy part of everyday life. For the empath, even the commute to and from a location, surrounded by the heightened emotions of traffic as well as passing through a multitude of energy waves exuded from other drivers, pedestrians or passing stores can be enough to send them right back home. The confines of a vehicle which may seem like a refuge of solitude for many introverts, turns into a chamber wrought with a continuous stream of energy bullets to the empath.

Some days feel almost impossible to function as a normal human in a world of others who appear so grounded and controlled, leaving the empathic INFJ to feel very alone in their daily struggles. For this reason, a support system is incredibly important. That support system can be other like-minded individuals that you were lucky enough to meet in person, a rare treat indeed, or an online group that becomes available with the click of a button. If more social interaction is the opposite of what you are looking for, websites and books that help you feel a little less alone are also a great everyday resource. When you are struggling, the thoughts in your head fuel you toward a downward spiral or they reassure and lift you up. Having handy resources that help remind you that you are not alone in how you perceive and handle the world is a great way to refocus your thoughts in a more positive manner.

When you need to head out for an errand, take a moment to read a few words from like-minded individuals, maybe even create a notebook that allows you to compile some of your favorite inspirational quotes from websites and books or use the space provided on page 21 of *The Empathic INFJ Workbook*.

After reading the inspirational words, take a moment to check in with your emotions before even walking out of your door. This will help prepare you to stay cognizant of the energies that you pick up upon leaving.

When you have the time and ability to recognize and mentally file away any foreign energies, it allows you to feel less overwhelmed when you are out and about. Only when these energies overtake you and feel impossible to pinpoint do you start to feel worn down. For this reason, stay aware of your emotions and the level of energy around you. If things start to feel out of control, that is when you need to allow yourself to leave the situation, even just sneaking to a restroom, to regain your sense of composure using the tools from your portable tool bag.

Your mental state as you excuse yourself is very important. If you are beating yourself up for needing to take some time in the midst of your day out, then you will struggle with rebalancing your energies as the negativity will overwhelm you. Instead, offer yourself some compassion. Remind yourself that you are dealing with a lot and your capacity is amazing. Mentally reward yourself for even leaving the house. Notice any negative self-talk and break it down to recognize the lie in the statements. Spin them around to see the positive truths.

Why do I have to be so sensitive? Because, despite the difficulty it may cause at the grocery store, it enables me to help others on a phenomenal level.

Everyone here thinks I'm crazy. Because they cannot possibly understand the weight of what I carry every day. If they could, they would see how amazingly strong I am.

I am so sick of being overwhelmed and tired all the time. So I will work harder on self-care and practicing the tools from my tool bag. Happiness, comfort and coping are well within my control.

Once you feel in control of your emotions, head back out and finish your responsibilities. You may find that your ability to cope while grow smaller and smaller the longer you are out, so focus on planning your days to limit your number of responsibilities at any given time. If you know you have a day with a lot of interaction through meetings at work, maybe put off your grocery shopping trip for another day. If you have four different stores you need to hit to finish your list, try splitting them up and doing two stores one day and two stores another. If you must overexert yourself and have little opportunity to take breaks, continually focus on your self-talk. Keep it positive and assess any negative. The more positive energy you produce yourself, the easier it becomes to handle negative energies that travel your way.

OBJECT AND ANIMAL EMPATH

While a lot of this section discusses handling energies from other humans, the fact is, many empathic INFJs are also object and animal empaths, absorbing energies emitted from the domesticated and wild animals around them as well as items in a room, store or even buildings themselves. For these empaths, there is little reprieve. Sneaking off to a restroom to escape human energies won't help much if you pick up on the energies of the room you are in.

If you believe you are an empath to either objects, animals, or both, take heart for you still can find locations to allow you to rebalance and cleanse yourself of these energies. It is important for you to find a consistent location that brings you peace. For some, they find this location within their own home, especially if they are the first owners of the building. Others who have older houses or reside in a busy apartment complex may never feel at peace in their homes, but instead seek solace at a remote park or wilderness area. Search around, checking in with yourself at different locations to decide where you feel the most comfortable and at peace. This may take some time but the reward will be well worth trying several locations. It is important to seek a spot that is convenient to your everyday living as opposed to one that would require a getaway or taking time out of life to reach. You want this space to be a piece of your tool bag.

Animal empaths might find some inconsistency in selecting a location. While most feel the positivity and comfort radiating from wildlife, suffering, pain and fear from animals can still dramatically affect their energy space. Depending on the intensity of the natural occurrence in or around your solitary refuge, one negative act can taint the space indefinitely. Stay aware of how you feel each time you seek solace in that space and if it feels like an energy is lingering, consider finding a new spot for your rebalancing. Smudging with sage, as previously mentioned, may also help cleanse the negative energy, allowing you to continue to enjoy your refuge.

Another thing to consider is to purchase new objects whenever possible. This helps to ensure that negative energies have not had a chance to attach to the object from previous ownership. If this is not a choice as it can be expensive to always purchase new, stay mindful of your used purchases. If something does not feel peaceful and balanced, no matter how much of a steal the price may be, your daily peace of mind might not be worth the savings.

Remember that being an object or animal empath also carries with it great joys of which others are unaware. Not all of the energies that you absorb will be negative meaning you have the capacity to enjoy some amazing positive experiences. A walk through a park may be peaceful for some, but you have the ability to tune in deeper to the energies of the plants and wildlife around you, taking in their carefree lives and basking in the comfort of their simplicity. For this reason, keeping a multitude of plants in your home or office can alter the energy of the space, filling it with positive energies for you take in all day long.

EMPATHIC INFJ RELATIONSHIPS

The empathic INFJ can struggle in social situations of all kinds, including simply entering a public place. They are bombarded with energy waves and absorb so much information through their intuition and empathic abilities that an everyday common experience becomes draining and overwhelming. For the most part, these everyday situations do not stay with the empath for long, especially if they are able to manage some time alone to recharge and rebalance their energy. But what happens when the empathic INFJ begins a relationship, gets married or even has children? How does the empath go from meeting people on an outing to living with another's energy?

This is where learning and understanding oneself is incredibly important. If you are not aware of nor fully understand your empathic abilities, your loved ones are sure to suffer, as are you. Let us look at some of the areas of struggle and why they may occur.

When it comes to living with loved ones, many introverts can seek refuge in a separate room, understanding their need to get away and recharge. The empath, however, does not necessarily have this simple luxury. Even if they are able to slip into the next room or perhaps manage to get out of the house, the energies of those dearest to them come along too.

Studies have been conducted that lend evidence to the distance one's energy waves can travel, just as Sheldrake's study mentioned earlier in this book. These energy waves are thought to be stronger when we are more in-tuned to another person and thus more familiar with their frequency. For this reason, even driving to the next county or state may not be enough to distance an empath from their loved ones' energies. This leaves many empaths perpetually exhausted, taking a toll on their health and their relationships.

As empaths, it is important to know that, despite the bombardment of energy waves we receive from others, we can take responsibility for our own emotions and establish boundaries for the emotional energies of those around us, including spouses, parents and children. In order to do this, we need to practice checking in with ourselves and understanding which emotions are our own and which belong to someone else. This is of utmost importance in any relationship to ensure that you do not become lost in another individual, which leads to codependency and encourages or creates abusive dynamics within relationships.

Once you have become more familiar with separating out emotions, you will be able to seek the solitude you need to recharge as an introvert while also being able to file away emotions that do not belong to you. This might prove challenging and lead to some empathic guilt, but recapturing who you are and taking time to focus only on your own emotions and self is not selfish. It is necessary to your mental health and well-being as well as the health of your relationships.

Relationships thrive when both parties have a healthy sense of self and well-defined boundaries. Since both self-definition and individuality are large areas of struggle and confusion for many empathic INFJs, it comes as no surprise that relationships carry with them a higher level of difficulty, even going as far as abusive and dysfunctional relationship patterns.

But by using the exercises and tools mentioned in the previous section, even the most empathic INFJ can establish their individuality and flourish in their relationship, with family, friends and romantic partners.

EMPATHIC CHILD

Very few empathic INFJs are lucky enough to have empathic parents who are fully aware of and understanding of their personal abilities. Even those who had or have an empathic parent probably recognize that parent's lack of knowledge about their abilities. Whether you are currently living with your parents or are reflecting back on your upbringing, it can help immensely to recognize the behaviors that may be holding you back in fully discovering and accepting your empathic gifts.

"You will never make it in this world if you don't toughen up."

"Why do you have to be so sensitive all the time?"

"I think you are being overly emotional."

"Maybe we should get you some help."

One or two, if not all of these phrases may ring familiar in your experience with your parents. They are all too common lines of thinking that leave the empathic child, in the height of discovering who they are, feeling shamed, saddened and broken. Even the best intentioned parents can let these types of phrases slip from time to time, usually during a particularly difficult time for the empathic child.

The shame that accompanies these statements causes the child to shift from figuring out who they are to defining themselves as wrong and putting their effort into fixing their perceived brokenness, stunting their emotional development which, in some, is never revisited and healed.

In order to move forward in understanding and accepting yourself, you must analyze these phrases and recognize the truths and lies within them. Let us take a moment now and break down these phrases, seeing what they really mean.

"You will never make it in this world if you don't toughen up." This is a lie. You are making it in this world, right now. Even if you are struggling and finding life difficult, as long as you are breathing, you are making it. There are so many out there just like you, sensitive, empathic INFJs, who are making it as well. Some of them, through embracing the very traits this statement wishes to tear down, are not only making it but they are thriving in this world. You do not need to toughen up to make it in this world.

"Why do you have to be so sensitive all the time?" This is more confusing because it is truth veiled with lying shame. You are sensitive. And you are sensitive all the time. There is nothing wrong with that. It is who you are genetically and physiologically. Feel free to cast the shame off this question and answer it authentically and proudly. Give them back the truth that lies within this question.

"I think you are being overly emotional." Another confusing phrase as it is opinion-based. They do genuinely think you are being overly emotional, which is

their truth. This does not make it your truth. "Overly emotional" is opinion, not fact. Everyone has varying levels of emotions in any given situation and you are bombarded with yours and those of the people around you. You are overflowing with emotions, but that does not make you "overly emotional." You are just as emotional as you should be.

"Maybe we should get you some help." This statement walks a fine line. Some parents are genuinely concerned watching their children struggle through aspects of life that others do not find so difficult. They may offer this truth with sincerity, allowing you the freedom to accept or deny. Remember that it should be your choice to seek help and there is nothing wrong with doing so. Other parents may use this as a judgment or your mental state. This is a lie. You may appear mentally unstable to those around you but inside you are stronger than they could imagine. You must be in order to handle the barrage of energy that overwhelms you each day. Accept assistance in your journey. Do not accept treatment for an issue that does not exist.

If your parents are still an active part of your life and making comments similar to those above, examine them, seek the truth and uncover the lies within the statements and answer them accordingly. You do not need to be disrespectful or cruel in your response, but standing up for your sensitivities and abilities will help you own who you are. Each time you stand up for yourself, it will get easier as you feel more and more empowered to be you, without shame.

On the other hand, if your parents are no longer a part of your life, whether through passing away or by choice, take some time to think through the statements they may have made in your past, upbringing or adulthood. As you analyze these statements, go ahead and respond to them just as you would if your parents stood before you. It might help to stand in front of a mirror and speak to the reflection as though it were your parent. Respond out loud, explaining to them that you are an empath and own your truths.

Facing the pieces of your upbringing that may have stunted your emotional growth and disallowed you to discover the full scope of your abilities will help you move forward, casting off the shame or judgments of those who do not experience life in the same way as you. As a teenager or adult, remind the empathic child within you that it is okay to be an empath and that you are strong and capable, regardless of what others may have told you.

EMPATHIC PARENT

As an empathic parent, it is easy to find yourself drained and struggling with emotional separation day in and day out. Children have very little control over their emotional state and, while some may find their tantrum over receiving the red cup instead of the blue one as tedious and unimportant, the empathic parent feels the genuine level of emotion this situation will bring up in their child, leaving them to feel the emotional rollercoaster full force all day long.

Parenting for a non-empath is considered one of the hardest jobs out there from an emotional point of view, from infancy all the way through the hormonal teen years. Unlike most intense situations, those involving your child usually do not allow you the chance to seek solitude. For the empathic parent, this emotionally challenging calling is amplified tenfold.

It is normal to want to ease your child's pains, worries and fears by jumping in and taking on responsibilities which should not fall on you. A parent's natural response is to help lessen negative emotions in their children, trying to make things better, and this response seems more amplified for the empathic parent who feels so intensely what their child is experiencing. But this does not help the child, nor does it lessen the suffering of the parent. An enabling relationship is detrimental to both parties and sets our children up for many future failures and disappointments.

In order to stop from being the ingrained super fixer you long to be, when absorbing the powerful emotions of your child, try not to act impulsively just to get the emotion in you to cease. Instead, identify the emotion, recognize it and accept it. Once you have done this, you can more easily focus yourself on the correct solution, working with your child in helping them understand and cope with their emotions. Taking a step back to assess the energy and situation, maybe taking a breath and counting to ten, will help you separate yourself from the strong energies you are picking up from your child. It also gives you a moment to determine whether or not you are acting out of love and guidance or empathic guilt.

Living in a house with others and being involved in any relationship as an empath is overwhelming and exhausting if we do not take the time to care for ourselves and release our empathic guilt. In order to not lose ourselves in the relationship, we have to understand the importance of labeling our emotions, assigning responsibility to each emotion and letting go of those energies that are not our responsibility.

EMPATHIC SPOUSE

The very nature of intimate romantic relationships is to give one's self completely to another, as well as to receive the other completely. When both are healthy and mature, with appropriately established trust, this transfer can be a beautiful thing. However, when insecurities, an unhealthy sense of self and an unbalanced ability to give enter the picture, the relationship stands on rocky ground, unable to allow love to grow.

This is often the case within an empathic's relationship as they have not been able to explore who they are, whether through lack of awareness and understanding or fear of seeing their personal truths,. Since they do not know who they are, they are left incapable of fully giving themselves to their partner. Instead, they give a fabrication or pieces of others that they have taken on as their own, making the relationship based on illusion instead of truth. We cannot fully love another unless we love ourselves and we cannot fully love ourselves unless we know ourselves.

Whether you are looking for love or currently in a relationship, it is never too late to apply the techniques in this book in order to gain a deeper understanding of yourself, allowing you to give yourself wholly to your partner, enhancing and deepening your capacity to love one another.

Even if you do fully understand yourself, it is important to not lose yourself in the relationship. Empaths have a tendency to absorb their partner's energies, losing their own self and emotionally burning out quickly in the relationship. This causes some to run from intimacy and others to jump into unhealthy relationship structures. The only way to combat this is to establish boundaries without external interference, especially from your significant other, which may blind your sight and make it harder for you to discover what matters most to you.

In order to do this, find a way to seek solitude for at least a few hours. Check in with yourself and your emotions, assigning ownership to each feeling, and allow yourself to temporarily box up what does not belong to you. From there, complete the boundaries exercise to decide your boundaries before coming back to your current relationship or starting a new one.

Let your spouse know ahead of time what you are doing. Perhaps even offer to have them read the boundaries section in this book. This will prepare them for your plans to be vocal and firm about your newly established boundaries and give you a safe place to strengthen them.

> If you are in a physically or emotionally abusive relationship, there is help and support available through the **National Domestic Violence Hotline**. 1-800-799-SAFE (7233) Or visit thehotline.org

If there are larger struggles or signs of abuse in your relationship which cause your spouse to fight against

113

your personal intentions to discover yourself and your boundaries, then consider seeking professional counsel. Setting personal boundaries is healthy, not to mention necessary, and you should never feel fearful or guilty of doing so. Remember the words of Drs. Cloud and Townsend: "The first thing you need to learn is that the person who is angry with you for setting boundaries is the one with the problem."[7]

Learning and understanding yourself, being able to distinguish between your emotions and your partner's and setting firm and clear boundaries will lead you to the deeper and more intimate romantic experience of which you are capable and deserving.

---

[7] Cloud, Henry, Ph.D. and John Townsend, Ph.D. *Boundaries: When to Say Yes, How to Say No to Take Control of Your Life.* Thomas Nelson Publishing. 1992.

CONCLUSION

Blake awoke one Tuesday morning after a night of internet browsing where he discovered the term empath. Though he was feeling fatigued from a late night of perusing website after website, fueled with excitement about learning all he could of what it meant to be an intuitive clairsentient, he felt rejuvenated and ready to start his day.

As Blake backed down his driveway toward the familiar stream of vehicles, his mood was met with stress, anxiety, anger and more. With each emotion that hit him, he wondered, *is this mine?*

Settling down in his cubicle, Blake felt intrigued about all the feelings running through him. Instead of assuming they belonged to him and allowing them to negatively taint the rest of his day, he noticed them, accepted them and was more aware than ever before of how they affected his actions.

Discovering what it meant to be an empathic INFJ changed Blake's outlook on life. As he crawled into bed that evening, he pondered the many energies he absorbed throughout the day, admiring with awe these abilities he has carried all along. Blake almost could not wait to begin the next day, excited to meet the many energies surrounding him.

As you can see, the empathic INFJ experiences life through a different lens than most. Their everyday involvements are filled with the energies of other people and objects around them making simple tasks muddled and complicated. Relationships feel confusing and exhausting and, before they know it, they are burnt out.

But simply by gaining awareness of the source of these everyday struggles, the empathic INFJ's life can turn around. Using the techniques described in this book, it is not only possible to find peace in your life but to thrive and enhance the lives of those around you.

Always remember that if you believe that you can control what comes into your emotional space, you will control it.

ALSO LOOK FOR

The Empathic INFJ Workbook:
Tools and Strategies for the Intuitive Clairsentient

This workbook, when paired with *The Empathic INFJ: Awareness and Understanding for the Intuitive Clairsentient* will offer you a functional and focused guide to understanding your empathic abilities and help you learn and establish new tools and techniques to thrive in your day to day living.

Complete with tests, worksheets and note pages, grab your copy today!

A Look Inside A Rare Mind:
An INFJ's Journal through Personal Discovery

A raw look into the mind of an INFJ through the beginning stages of her journey from first discovering her Myers-Briggs Personality Type.

This book is a descriptive personal journal shared to help those who are at the beginning stages of discovering that they, too, are an INFJ and may be searching for validation, understanding and a kindred spirit.

For more information about these works as well as future publications, please visit jennifersoldner.com

Printed in Great Britain
by Amazon